contents

welcome   3

chef's tips   4

starters & salads   6

meat & poultry dishes   30

fish dishes   58

rice, lentils & pulses   70

vegetable dishes   86

desserts   104

index   118

curry heaven

50 amazing creations for curry lovers!

Curry is officially the UK's favourite meal – and the great news is that it doesn't need to be off the menu when you're losing weight with Slimming World. Now you can make your favourite curries at home for a fraction of the cost and Syns of a takeaway or ready meal with our new '**Curry Heaven**' cookbook.

These authentic Indian dishes cover everything from starters such as onion bhajis and vegetable samosas, hot and spicy meat dishes like classic chicken curry and beef madras and fantastic fish recipes including Kerala-style fish and tandoori monkfish to rice and vegetable dishes such as classic pilau rice and aloo gobi. Whether you prefer to spend as little time as possible in the kitchen or you're happy to linger over a special dish, you'll find recipes to suit you. You can share your curry creations with family and friends and they'll never know that you're slimming.

Most of the recipes are completely Free, so you can eat and enjoy without ever feeling hungry. With **Curry Heaven**, you can fill your weight loss journey with Indian inspired meals the whole family will love.

chef's tips

stock

Where stock is mentioned in a recipe, you can use any of the following as they are all Free: all varieties of stock cubes, bouillon cubes/powder, ready-to-use liquid stock, and liquid stock concentrate. Please note that gravy granules or powder and stock granules are not Free.

spoon-wise

Unless you measure food accurately, it's very easy to go over your intended Syn intake without realising it. (For instance, 1 level tablespoon of cornflour is 3½ Syns, 1 rounded tablespoon counts as 5 Syns.) To get an accurate level spoon measure, scrape a knife along the top of the spoon, knocking the excess food back into its container. For accuracy and ease, we'd recommend investing in a set of measuring spoons.

low calorie cooking spray

To cut down on fat in recipes, we recommend using non-stick cookware/bakeware wherever possible. However, if you do need to use fat then choose a low calorie cooking spray which contains 2 calories or less per spray.

fat free natural fromage frais and yogurt

These are wonderful ingredients for cooks as they give the creamy texture and taste normally achieved with cream. However, when boiled they tend to separate and can make the dish look unappetising. Add them at the end, once all the other ingredients have been cooked, and simply heat through. This works brilliantly if you want your curry a touch milder or creamier.

Top tip: If you have favourite recipes at home that use cream, it's normally possible to replace this with fromage frais or yogurt and still achieve equally tasty results.

trimming meat and poultry

It's a good idea to trim any visible fat from meat and remove the skin from poultry before you cook it, then you won't be tempted to eat it when it's cooked.

suitable for vegetarians?

Many of the recipes in this book are suitable for vegetarians. Any recipes containing meat, fish or poultry can be made vegetarian by replacing these ingredients with your choice of Free Quorn, textured vegetable protein/soya protein or tofu.

fruit Syn values

Reading through the recipes, you'll notice that some that contain fruit have been given a Syn value. Fruit is given a Syn value when it is juiced, cooked, puréed, mashed, stewed or blended because it becomes very easy to over consume. Eating fruit that has been juiced, cooked, puréed etc, is a very effective way of adding a lot of extra energy in a non-filling form and your appetite isn't satisfied in the same way as eating fresh whole fruit.

serves...

shows how many people/portions the recipe serves

freezer friendly

indicates which recipes can be safely frozen for up to 1 month

ready in...

tells how long the recipe takes to make including preparation and cooking times

curry heaven
spice rack!

Most of the recipes in this book are flavoured with an array of different herbs and spices, many of which will be familiar to curry aficionados. It may look daunting at first but you will find you'll use a few key spices again and again. To help with your shopping, here's a list of the all the herbs and spices used in the recipes.

fresh staples

Red and green chillies, coriander, garlic, lemon grass, mint and root ginger.

storecupboard staples

Bay leaves, black mustard seeds, black peppercorns, cardamom pods and seeds, cayenne pepper, chilli powder (mild, medium, hot), cinnamon (ground and sticks), cloves (ground and whole), coriander (ground and seeds), cumin (ground and seeds), curry powder (mild, medium, hot), dried red chillies, dried mint, fennel seeds, garam masala, ground ginger, nam pla (Thai fish sauce), nutmeg, paprika, tandoori spice powder and turmeric.

unusual ingredients

Amchoor (dried mango powder), chat masala, fresh curry leaves, galangal, kaffir lime leaves, saffron threads and tamarind paste.

starters
& salads

coconut chicken soup

serves 4
each serving is:
1 Syn on Extra Easy
1 Syn on Original
5 Syns on Green

freezer friendly
ready in 45 minutes

2 x 150g skinless and boneless
chicken breasts

4 kaffir lime leaves, finely shredded*

2 tbsp very finely chopped lemon grass

1 tsp peeled and very finely
grated galangal*

700ml chicken stock

juice of 1 lime

6 tbsp very finely chopped coriander

2 tsp nam pla (Thai fish sauce)*

1 red chilli, deseeded and very
finely sliced

4 tbsp reduced fat coconut milk

4 spring onions, trimmed and very
finely sliced

salt and freshly ground black pepper

Place the chicken, kaffir lime leaves, lemon grass, galangal and chicken stock in a medium saucepan and bring to the boil.

Reduce the heat to low, cover and simmer gently for 20-25 minutes or until the chicken is cooked through. Using a slotted spoon, remove the chicken from the saucepan and tear the flesh into bite-sized shreds with your fingers.

Return the chicken to the saucepan with the lime juice, chopped coriander, nam pla, red chilli, coconut milk and most of the spring onions. Season well and heat gently for 4-5 minutes until warmed through. Serve immediately garnished with the remaining spring onion.

The kaffir lime leaves can be replaced with the zest of two limes; the galangal with root ginger; and the nam pla with light soy sauce.

curried parsnip soup

serves 6
each serving is:
Free on Extra Easy
Free on Green
4 Syns on Original

freezer friendly
vegetarian
ready in 1 hour 30 minutes

2 onions, peeled and chopped

low calorie cooking spray

2 garlic cloves, peeled and crushed

1 tbsp mild curry powder

1 tsp ground cumin

1 tsp turmeric

1 tsp ground coriander

1 tsp ground ginger

1.2 litres vegetable stock

700g parsnips, peeled and diced

salt and freshly ground black pepper

a dash of Tabasco sauce (optional)

a pinch of cayenne pepper

fresh oregano, to serve

Fry the onions in a little low calorie cooking spray until softened. Add the garlic, curry powder and spices and fry for a further 3 minutes, adding a little stock if the mixture becomes too dry.

Add the parsnips and stock to the pan and bring to the boil. Reduce the heat to a simmer and cook gently for about an hour. Remove the pan from the heat and allow to cool a little.

Transfer the soup to a food processor, season well and blend until smooth. Return the soup to the pan, add a dash of Tabasco if you like it hot, reheat gently and served garnished with a pinch of cayenne pepper and a few springs of fresh oregano.

lamb koftas
with mint relish

serves 4
each serving is:
2½ Syns on Extra Easy
2½ Syns on Original
14 Syns on Green

freezer friendly
ready in 45 minutes

600g lean lamb leg steaks, roughly cubed or chopped

1 red onion, peeled and finely chopped

2 garlic cloves, peeled and crushed

a small handful each of fresh coriander and mint, finely chopped

1 tsp each of ground ginger, mild chilli powder and ground cumin

2 tsp roughly crushed coriander seeds

1 egg, beaten

salt and freshly ground black pepper

50g breadcrumbs

lime wedges, to serve

for the mint relish

1 onion, peeled and finely chopped

2 tomatoes, finely chopped

½ cucumber, finely chopped

150g fat free natural yogurt

4 tbsp chopped mint

juice of 1 lime

First make the relish by mixing all the relish ingredients together in a bowl, cover and chill until needed.

Preheat the oven to 200°C/Gas 6.

Place the cubed lamb in a food processor with the onion, garlic, chopped coriander and mint, ground ginger, chilli powder, ground cumin, crushed coriander seeds and the egg. Season well and process until fairly smooth and well combined.

Divide the mixture into 16 balls. Roll each ball in the breadcrumbs, place on a baking tray and cook for 15-20 minutes, or until cooked through.

Serve the lamb koftas on cocktail sticks with the mint relish and a wedge of lime to squeeze over.

tandoori
chicken

serves 4
each serving is:
Free on Extra Easy
Free on Original
11 Syns on Green

ready in 15 minutes

juice of 1 lime

2 tbsp tandoori spice powder

2 tbsp fat free natural yogurt

8 large chicken drumsticks, skinless

salt and freshly ground black pepper

low calorie cooking spray

6 mixed peppers, deseeded and sliced into strips

1 tbsp red wine vinegar

mixed salad leaves and lime wedges, to serve

Place the lime juice in a bowl and mix with the tandoori spice powder and yogurt. Make a few deep cuts in each drumstick with a sharp knife and spread the spicy yogurt mixture onto the chicken, making sure it gets into the flesh. Season and spray with low calorie cooking spray.

Place the drumsticks under a hot grill and cook for 10-12 minutes, turning until cooked through. Cover and keep warm.

Meanwhile, place the pepper strips in a bowl with the red wine vinegar, spray with low calorie cooking spray, season well and toss to mix. Heat a griddle and cook the peppers for 3-4 minutes until tender and slightly charred. Serve the drumsticks with the peppers and accompany with mixed salad leaves and lime wedges to squeeze over.

grilled
tiger prawns

serves 4
each serving is:
Free on Extra Easy
Free on Original
4½ Syns on Green

ready in 15 minutes plus marinating

450g raw tiger prawns, peeled but
with the tails left on

1 garlic clove, peeled and crushed

1 green chilli, deseeded and chopped

juice of ½ lime

1.5cm piece root ginger, peeled
and grated

150g fat free natural yogurt

1 tsp garam masala

salt and freshly ground black pepper

salad leaves and lime wedges, to serve

Cut each prawn in half lengthways down to the tail so that the prawns fan out. Thread onto 8 skewers and place in a shallow dish.

Mix the remaining ingredients together, spoon over the prawn kebabs and leave to marinate in the fridge for 20-30 minutes.

Remove the prawns from the marinade and cook under a hot grill for 2-3 minutes on each side. They will turn pink when they are cooked. Serve with salad leaves and lime wedges.

masala crab cakes

serves 4
each serving is:
Free on Extra Easy
Free on Original
5 Syns on Green

freezer friendly
ready in 35 minutes plus chilling

200g fresh white crab meat

200g skinless white fish fillet
(cod or halibut), roughly chopped

1 tbsp mild curry powder

2 garlic cloves, peeled and crushed

1 red chilli, deseeded and finely chopped

4 tbsp peeled and finely chopped
red onion

4 tbsp chopped coriander, plus a
little to garnish

1 small egg, beaten

salt and freshly ground black pepper

low calorie cooking spray

finely chopped red pepper, lemon wedges
and fat free natural yogurt, to serve

Place the crab meat, white fish, curry powder, garlic, red chilli, red onion, chopped coriander and egg in a food processor. Season well and process for a few seconds until well mixed. Transfer to a mixing bowl and cover and chill in the fridge for 5-6 hours (or overnight if time permits) to allow the mixture to firm up and let the flavours combine.

Preheat the oven to 200°C/Gas 6. Line a baking sheet with non-stick baking parchment and spray with low calorie cooking spray. Divide the crab mixture into 12 portions and shape each one into a 'cake'.

Place on the prepared baking sheet and bake for 20-25 minutes or until lightly browned and cooked through. Serve immediately garnished with chopped coriander, red pepper and lemon wedges, with the yogurt on the side to dip into.

curry heaven starters & salads

onion bhajis

makes 12
each bhaji is:
1 Syn on Extra Easy
1 Syn on Green
1 Syn on Original

freezer friendly
vegetarian
ready in 30 minutes plus resting

200g onions, peeled, halved and
thinly sliced

60g gram flour (chickpea flour)

1 tsp lemon juice

2 tsp ground cumin

1 tbsp coriander seeds, crushed

1 tsp deseeded and chopped green chilli

1 tbsp chopped coriander

¼ level tsp baking powder

salt

low calorie cooking spray

a pinch of paprika

Place the onions, gram flour, lemon juice, ground cumin, coriander seeds, green chilli, chopped coriander and baking powder in a mixing bowl. Season with salt and add a few tablespoons of water to form a thick batter that coats the onion. Leave to rest for 15 minutes and then, using your fingers, mix again to combine thoroughly.

Preheat the oven to 220°C/Gas 7. Line a baking sheet with baking parchment and, using your fingers or a dessert spoon, drop small mounds of the mixture onto the prepared baking sheet to give you 12 bhajis.

Spray with low calorie cooking spray and bake for 15-20 minutes until golden. Remove from the heat and serve immediately sprinkled with a little paprika.

vegetable samosas
with hara chutney

makes 18
each samosa is:
1 Syn on Extra Easy
1 Syn on Green
2 Syns on Original

freezer friendly
vegetarian
ready in 55 minutes

low calorie cooking spray

1 tbsp mild curry powder and
1 tsp amchoor (dried mango powder)*

400g potatoes, peeled, boiled
and mashed

110g frozen peas

4 tbsp finely chopped coriander

1 red chilli, deseeded and finely chopped

salt

3 large filo pastry sheets (24 x 50cm)

for the hara chutney
110g fresh coriander and
50g fresh mint, finely chopped

1 tsp peeled and finely grated root ginger
and 2 green chillies, deseeded and
finely chopped

juice of 2 limes

2 tsp sea salt and ¼ tsp artificial sweetener

Place all the chutney ingredients in a food processor with 75ml of water and blend until smooth. Set aside until needed.

Spray a large non-stick frying pan with low calorie cooking spray and place over a medium heat. Add the curry powder, amchoor, potatoes and peas and stir-fry for 4-5 minutes. Remove from the heat and add the chopped coriander and red chilli, season well with salt and set aside.

Preheat the oven to 190°C/Gas 5. Line a large baking sheet with baking parchment. Working swiftly, place the three filo sheets on top of each other and cut them in half widthways. Then cut each half into three even strips lengthways to give you a total of six strips of filo per sheet (18 strips in total).

Lay the strips on a clean work surface and lightly spray with low calorie cooking spray. Place a teaspoonful of the potato filling at the bottom of each strip and fold the pastry diagonally to enclose the filling and form a triangle. Press down on the pastry and fold again until you reach the end of the strip leaving you with a triangular pastry parcel. Repeat with the remaining strips and filling to make 18 parcels.

Place the parcels in a single layer on the prepared baking sheet, spray with low calorie cooking spray and bake for 15-20 minutes or until golden and crisp. Remove from the oven and serve warm with the hara chutney.

Amchoor is available from larger supermarkets and Asian greengrocers.

meaty citrus salad

serves 4
each serving is:
½ **Syn** on Extra Easy
½ **Syn** on Original
4½ **Syns** on Green

ready in 20 minutes

low calorie cooking spray

1 small onion, peeled and very
finely chopped

2 garlic cloves, peeled and
very finely chopped

1 tsp peeled and finely grated root ginger

2 tsp medium curry powder

250g extra lean minced beef

salt and freshly ground black pepper

juice of 1 orange

2 large oranges, peeled and segmented

2 little gem lettuces, leaves separated

red pepper strips, to serve

Spray a large pan with low calorie cooking spray and place over a medium heat. Add the onion, garlic and ginger and stir-fry for 3-4 minutes.

Add the curry powder and minced beef and stir-fry over a high heat for 5-6 minutes or until the beef is browned and cooked through. Remove from the heat and season well. Stir in the orange juice and allow to cool.

Meanwhile, divide the orange segments and lettuce leaves between four serving plates. Top with the beef mixture, garnish with red pepper strips and serve immediately.

lemon grass
prawn salad

serves 4
each serving is:
Free on Extra Easy
Free on Original
2 Syns on Green

ready in 20 minutes

50ml chicken stock

2 tbsp nam pla (Thai fish sauce)

2 tsp mild or medium curry powder

24 raw tiger prawns, peeled but with
the tails left on

1 tbsp very finely chopped lemon grass

3 small shallots, peeled and very
finely chopped

¼ tsp artificial sweetener

2 tbsp lemon juice

2 spring onions, trimmed and
finely chopped

1 small cucumber, cut into thin shreds
using a vegetable peeler

1 carrot, peeled and cut into thin shreds
using a vegetable peeler

light soy sauce, to serve

Place the stock, nam pla and curry powder in a saucepan and bring to the boil. Add the prawns and cook for 3-4 minutes or until opaque and just cooked through.

Add the remaining ingredients, stir and cook for 1 minute and then remove from the heat.

Divide the salad between four bowls and serve immediately with light soy sauce to drizzle over.

aloo chat

serves 4
each serving is:
Free on Extra Easy
Free on Green
4 Syns on Original

vegetarian
ready in 20 minutes plus chilling

for the chat masala*

1 tbsp freshly ground black pepper

2 tbsp sea salt

1 tbsp dry-roasted cumin seeds,
roughly ground

3 tsp amchoor (dried mango powder)**

1 tsp mild or medium chilli powder

for the aloo

1 red apple, cored and cut into
small cubes

3 medium potatoes, peeled, boiled and
cut into small cubes

1 small cucumber, cut into small cubes

juice of 1 lemon

4 tsp chat masala

a handful of chopped coriander and mint

Mix all the chat masala ingredients together and store in an airtight container until needed.

To make the aloo, place the apple, potatoes, cucumber and lemon juice into a mixing bowl and sprinkle over the chat masala. Toss to mix well and cover and chill in the fridge for 30 minutes to allow the flavours and the spices to develop.

Toss in the chopped herbs and mix well.
Serve immediately.

The chat masala can be made and stored in an airtight container for up to 1 month. Alternatively, you can buy it ready-made from larger supermarkets and Asian greengrocers.

**Amchoor is available from larger supermarkets and Asian greengrocers.*

meat
& poultry
dishes

beef kofta curry

serves 4
each serving is:
Free on Extra Easy
Free on Original
11½ Syns on Green

freezer friendly
ready in 40 minutes

700g extra lean minced beef

2 tsp peeled and finely grated root ginger

2 garlic cloves, peeled and crushed

2 tsp crushed fennel seeds

1 tsp ground cinnamon

1 tsp mild or medium chilli powder

salt and freshly ground black pepper

1 tsp turmeric

2 tbsp medium curry powder

500g passata

¼ tsp artificial sweetener

fat free natural yogurt, chilli powder and mint leaves, to serve

Place the minced beef in a mixing bowl along with the ginger, garlic, fennel seeds, ground cinnamon and chilli powder. Season and, using your hands, mix thoroughly until well combined. Form the mixture into small, walnut-sized balls and set aside.

Place the turmeric, curry powder, passata and sweetener in a medium saucepan and bring to the boil. Reduce the heat to a simmer, season well and carefully place the meatballs in the sauce. Cover and cook gently for 15-20 minutes, turning the meatballs occasionally, until they are cooked through.

Remove from the heat and serve drizzled with the yogurt, sprinkled with a pinch of chilli powder and garnished with the mint leaves.

beef madras

serves 4
each serving is:
Free on Extra Easy
Free on Original
14½ Syns on Green

freezer friendly
ready in 2 hours

low calorie cooking spray

1 onion, peeled and finely chopped

4 cloves and 6 cardamom pods

2 fresh red chillies, deseeded and finely chopped

1 tsp peeled and finely grated root ginger

2 garlic cloves, peeled and crushed

2 dried red chillies

1 tbsp medium or hot curry powder

900g casserole beef or braising steak, all visible fat removed, cut into bite-sized chunks

2 tsp ground coriander and 1 tsp ground cumin

250ml beef stock

salt

chopped coriander, to garnish

boiled rice, to serve (optional)

Spray a saucepan liberally with low calorie cooking spray and place over a medium heat. Add the onion, cloves and cardamom pods and stir-fry for 3-4 minutes.

Add the fresh chillies, ginger, garlic and dried chillies and stir-fry for a further 2 minutes.

Add the curry powder and beef chunks to the saucepan and stir-fry for 6-8 minutes until the meat is sealed.

Add the ground coriander and cumin, and stock and bring to the boil. Season with salt, cover tightly and reduce the heat to low. Cook gently for 1½ hours, stirring occasionally, until the meat is tender. Remove the pan from the heat and scatter over some chopped coriander.

Delicious served with freshly boiled rice, if wished.

dahiwalla ghosht
with kachumber

serves 4
each serving is:
Free on Extra Easy
Free on Original
23 Syns on Green

freezer friendly
ready in 45 minutes plus overnight marinating

4 trimmed racks of lamb

3 garlic cloves, peeled and crushed

2 tsp peeled and finely grated root ginger

2 tbsp white wine vinegar

2 tbsp dried mint, 3 tsp ground cumin,
2 tsp ground coriander and 1 tsp mild
chilli powder

150g fat free natural yogurt

salt and freshly ground black pepper

for the kachumber

1 cucumber, peeled, deseeded and
finely diced

4 firm tomatoes, deseeded and
finely diced

½ onion, peeled and finely diced

4 tbsp chopped coriander and
2 tbsp chopped mint

juice of 2 limes

Place the racks of lamb in a single layer in a shallow bowl. Place all the remaining ingredients in a food processor, season well and blend until smooth. Pour this mixture over the lamb to coat evenly. Cover and leave to marinate overnight in the fridge to allow the flavours to develop.

Remove the lamb from the fridge 1 hour before cooking. Preheat the oven to 200°C/Gas 6, place the lamb on a non-stick baking sheet and bake for 20-25 minutes or until cooked to your liking.

Meanwhile make the kachumber: place all the ingredients in a bowl, season well and stir to mix. Stand at room temperature for 10-15 minutes to allow the flavours to develop.

Remove the lamb from the oven, cover with foil and allow to rest for 5-10 minutes before carving each rack into cutlets. Serve immediately with the kachumber.

Tip: *If you can't find trimmed racks of lamb, ask your local butcher to 'French trim' them for you.*

lamb
rogan josh

serves 4
each serving is:
Free on Extra Easy
Free on Original
8½ Syns on Green

freezer friendly
ready in 50 minutes

1 onion, peeled and chopped

3 garlic cloves, peeled and chopped

low calorie cooking spray

1 tsp each of ground coriander, paprika,
ground ginger and chilli powder

450g lamb steaks, all visible fat removed,
cut into bite-sized pieces

400g can chopped tomatoes

1 bay leaf

2 x 2.5cm pieces of cinnamon stick

4 cardamom pods

3 cloves

200ml chicken stock

2 tsp artificial sweetener

a small handful fresh coriander, chopped

mangetout, to serve

Fry the onion and garlic in low calorie cooking spray until soft. Add all the powdered spices and fry for 1 minute (add a little water if it gets too dry).

Add the lamb, tomatoes, bay leaf, cinnamon sticks, cardamom pods, cloves, stock and sweetener and simmer for 30-35 minutes until reduced.

Remove the bay leaf and cinnamon sticks. Stir in the chopped coriander and serve immediately with freshly steamed mangetout.

lamb dhansak

serves 4
each serving is:
Free on Extra Easy
4 Syns on Original
11½ Syns on Green

freezer friendly
ready in 2 hours 15 minutes

100g dried red lentils

500g carrots, peeled and cut
into large chunks

2 onions, peeled and thinly sliced

400g can chopped tomatoes

1 tsp turmeric

1 tbsp ground cumin

2 tsp ground coriander

2 tsp finely crushed cardamom seeds

low calorie cooking spray

600g lean lamb leg steaks, cubed

2 tsp peeled and finely grated root ginger

6 garlic cloves, peeled and crushed

3 red chillies, deseeded and finely sliced

2 tsp garam masala

4 tbsp chopped coriander

Put the lentils, carrots, onions and tomatoes in a pan with the turmeric, ground cumin, ground coriander and cardamom seeds. Add enough water to just cover the lentils and vegetables, then simmer gently for about 25-30 minutes or until the lentils are tender.

Spray a non-stick pan with low calorie cooking spray and place over a high heat. Add the lamb in batches and brown all over. Add the ginger, garlic and red chillies. Cook for a few minutes then add the lentil mixture along with 200ml of water.

Cover and simmer for 1½ hours (remove cover for final 30 minutes), or until the lamb is completely tender and the sauce is thickened. Stir in the garam masala and chopped coriander and serve immediately.

kheema with curry leaves

serves 4
each serving is:
Free on Extra Easy
Free on Original
7 Syns on Green

ready in 35 minutes

low calorie cooking spray

1 large onion, peeled and finely chopped

10-12 fresh curry leaves*

2 green chillies, deseeded and chopped

400g extra lean turkey breast mince

3 garlic cloves, peeled and crushed

1 tsp peeled and finely grated root ginger

1 tsp mild chilli powder

¼ tsp turmeric

1 tsp salt

2 ripe tomatoes, quartered

4 tbsp chopped coriander

Spray a frying pan with low calorie cooking spray and place over a medium heat. Add the onion, curry leaves and green chillies and stir-fry for 2-3 minutes.

Place the turkey mince in a bowl along with the garlic, ginger, chilli powder, turmeric and salt. Mix thoroughly using your fingers. Add this mixture to the frying pan and stir-fry over a high heat for 7-10 minutes.

Add the tomatoes and chopped coriander and continue to fry for 3-4 minutes. Remove from the heat and serve.

If you can't find fresh curry leaves, use 1-2 bay leaves instead.

pork vindaloo

serves 4
each serving is:
Free on Extra Easy
Free on Original
8 Syns on Green

freezer friendly
ready in 1 hour 30 minutes plus marinating

500g pork steaks, all visible fat removed,
cut into bite-sized chunks

125ml vinegar

1 onion, peeled and grated

2 tsp each of ground cumin and ground
black mustard seeds

8 garlic cloves, peeled and crushed

2 tsp peeled and finely grated root ginger

1 tsp hot chilli powder

½ tsp ground cloves

1 tsp ground cinnamon

400g can chopped tomatoes

¼ tsp artificial sweetener

salt and freshly ground black pepper

chopped coriander, to serve

Place the pork in a bowl, mix 1 tablespoon of the vinegar with a little water and pour over the pork, turning until throughly coated.

Place the remaining vinegar in a bowl with the onion, ground cumin, mustard seeds, garlic, ginger, chilli powder, ground cloves and cinnamon. Mix well to form a smooth paste and pour over the pork to coat evenly. Cover the bowl and leave to marinate in the fridge for 6-8 hours (or overnight if time permits).

Add 200ml of water to a pan along with the pork mixture, tomatoes and sweetener and bring to the boil. Reduce the heat to low, season well, cover tightly and simmer gently for about an hour or until the pork is tender.

Remove from the heat and allow to rest for 10 minutes before serving with the chopped coriander scattered over.

classic chicken curry

serves 4
each serving is:
Free on Extra Easy
Free on Original
13½ Syns on Green

freezer friendly
ready in 1 hour 10 minutes

1kg skinless and boneless chicken thighs or breasts, cut into large pieces

salt and freshly ground black pepper

low calorie cooking spray

1 onion, peeled and finely chopped

2 tsp peeled and finely grated root ginger

2 tsp peeled and crushed garlic

1 tbsp mild or medium curry powder

1 tsp each of ground cumin, ground coriander, ground cinnamon and paprika

½ tsp crushed cardamom seeds and ¼ tsp each of ground cloves and turmeric

400g can chopped tomatoes

300ml chicken stock

chopped coriander, sliced green chillies and fat free natural yogurt, to serve

Place the chicken on a plate, season well and set aside.

Spray a frying pan with low calorie cooking spray and place over a medium heat. Add the onion and stir-fry for 5-6 minutes or until starting to lightly brown.

Stir in the ginger, garlic, curry powder, cumin, coriander, cinnamon, paprika, cardamom seeds, ground cloves and turmeric and stir-fry over a high heat for 1-2 minutes.

Add the chicken and cook for 2-3 minutes until sealed, then add the tomatoes and stock. Bring to the boil, cover tightly, reduce the heat to low and allow to simmer gently for 40-45 minutes, stirring occasionally, until the chicken is cooked through.

Remove the frying pan from the heat, adjust the seasoning to taste and serve garnished with chopped coriander and sliced green chillies. If you enjoy a creamier curry or want to make the curry less hot swirl in some fat free natural yogurt.

jalfrezi
chicken

serves 4
each serving is:
Free on Extra Easy
Free on Original
8 Syns on Green

freezer friendly
ready in 45 minutes

4 x 150g skinless and boneless
chicken breasts

low calorie cooking spray

1 tsp cumin seeds

1 onion, peeled and finely sliced

1 red pepper and 1 yellow pepper,
deseeded and thinly sliced

2 garlic cloves, peeled and crushed and
1 tsp peeled and finely grated root ginger

1 tbsp medium curry powder, ½ tsp mild
or medium chilli powder and 1 tsp each
of ground cumin and ground coriander

salt and freshly ground black pepper

400g can chopped tomatoes

a large handful of chopped coriander

fat free natural yogurt and chopped
cucumber, to serve

Place the chicken breasts between sheets of cling film and flatten with a rolling pin. Remove the cling film, cut the chicken into thin strips and set aside.

Spray a large frying pan with low calorie cooking spray, place over a medium heat, add the cumin seeds and stir-fry for 1-2 minutes. Add the onion, peppers, garlic and ginger and fry for a further 6-8 minutes.

Add the curry powder, chilli powder, ground cumin and coriander. Season well and fry for 1-2 minutes.

Throw in the chicken, increase the heat to high and stir-fry for 4-5 minutes. Stir in the tomatoes and chopped coriander along with 100ml of water. Cover, reduce the heat to low and cook gently for about 15 minutes or until the chicken is tender. Remove from the heat, adjust the seasoning to taste and serve immediately with a bowl of yogurt and chopped cucumber.

shahi murgh

serves 4
each serving is:
Free on Extra Easy
Free on Original
13½ Syns on Green

freezer friendly
ready in 1 hour plus standing

salt and freshly ground black pepper

1kg skinless chicken thighs or breasts

250g fat free natural yogurt

2 tsp ground cumin

2 tsp ground coriander

¼ tsp mild chilli powder

5 tbsp chopped coriander

low calorie cooking spray

10 cardamom pods

8 cloves

2 cinnamon sticks

3 bay leaves

Season the chicken and set aside. Place the yogurt in a bowl and lightly beat until smooth. Season with salt and pepper, then add the ground cumin and coriander, chilli powder and chopped coriander, mix well and set aside.

Spray a large frying pan liberally with low calorie cooking spray and place over a high heat. Add the cardamom pods, cloves, cinnamon sticks and bay leaves and fry for 1-2 minutes. Add the chicken in a single layer and brown on both sides. Pour over the yogurt mixture, stir well, turn the heat to low, cover tightly and simmer gently for 20-25 minutes, stirring occasionally.

Uncover and cook for a further 3-4 minutes until the sauce thickens and coats the chicken. Remove from the heat and allow to stand for 5 minutes before serving.

chicken tikka masala

serves 4
each serving is:
1 Syn on Extra Easy
1 Syn on Original
9 Syns on Green

ready in 1 hour plus marinating

4 x 150g skinless chicken breasts,
cut into chunks

juice of 1 lime

150g fat free natural yogurt

1-2 drops of red food colouring (optional)

5 tbsp tikka curry powder

salt and freshly ground black pepper

low calorie cooking spray

1 onion, peeled and grated

4 garlic cloves, peeled and crushed

2.5cm piece root ginger, peeled
and grated

1 red chilli, deseeded and chopped

1 tsp each of ground cinnamon and
ground cumin

6 level tbsp tomato purée

5 tbsp fat free natural fromage frais

rice and vegetables or salad,
to serve (optional)

Place the chicken in a bowl. Mix the lime juice with the yogurt, food colouring, if using, and 3 tablespoons of the tikka curry powder. Season and pour over chicken. Toss to coat the chicken, cover and marinate in the fridge for 2-3 hours (or overnight if time permits).

Heat a frying pan sprayed with low calorie cooking spray. Add the onion and fry for 5-6 minutes. Add the garlic, ginger, red chilli, cinnamon, cumin and remaining curry powder and fry for 2-3 minutes. Stir in the tomato purée and 250ml of water. Bring to the boil, reduce the heat and simmer for 12-15 minutes, stirring often.

Meanwhile, thread the chicken onto eight metal skewers, spray with low calorie cooking spray and grill under a medium heat for 12-15 minutes, turning once or twice, until cooked through. Remove the chicken from the skewers and stir into the sauce. Take the sauce off the heat and stir in the fromage frais.

Delicious served with rice and vegetables or salad of your choice.

creamy
chicken korma

serves 4
each serving is:
Free on Extra Easy
Free on Original
13½ Syns on Green

freezer friendly
ready in 45 minutes

low calorie cooking spray

3 bay leaves

1 cinnamon stick

1 tsp crushed cardamom seeds, ¼ tsp
crushed cloves and 2 tsp cumin seeds

1 onion, peeled and finely grated

1 tbsp each of ground coriander and
ground cumin and 2 tsp mild curry powder

3 tsp peeled and finely grated root ginger
and 3 tsp peeled and finely crushed garlic

200g can chopped tomatoes

1kg skinless and boneless chicken
breasts, cut into bite-sized pieces

200ml chicken stock

salt and freshly ground black pepper

5 tbsp fat free natural fromage frais

freshly chopped mint, to garnish

Spray a large frying pan with low calorie cooking
spray and place over a high heat. Add the bay leaves,
cinnamon stick, cardamom seeds, cloves, cumin
seeds and onion and stir-fry for 5-6 minutes.

Add the ground coriander and cumin, curry powder,
ginger, garlic and tomatoes and stir-fry for another
3-4 minutes.

Put the chicken into the pan and pour over the
stock. Bring to the boil, season well, cover tightly,
reduce the heat to low and allow to simmer gently
for 20-25 minutes, stirring occasionally.

Remove the pan from the heat and stir in the fromage
frais. Serve immediately garnished with chopped mint.

turkey
shami kebabs

serves 4
each serving is:
Free on Extra Easy
Free on Original
14 Syns on Green

freezer friendly
ready in 35 minutes plus chilling

800g extra lean turkey breast mince

1 small red onion, peeled and finely grated

1 tsp peeled and finely grated root ginger

1 tbsp medium curry powder

1 tsp finely grated lime zest

1 red chilli, deseeded and finely chopped

3 tbsp chopped coriander

2 tbsp chopped mint

2 tbsp fat free natural yogurt

salt and freshly ground black pepper

low calorie cooking spray

red onion rings and lime wedges, to serve

Place the turkey mince in a mixing bowl with the onion, ginger, curry powder, lime zest, red chilli, chopped coriander and mint, and the yogurt. Season well and, using your hands, mix until well combined. Cover and chill in the fridge for 6-8 hours (or overnight if time permits) to allow the flavours to develop.

Preheat the oven to 200°C/Gas 6. Divide the turkey mixture into 12 portions and shape each portion into a flat, oval kebab shape. Place on a baking sheet lined with baking parchment and spray with low calorie cooking spray. Bake for 15-20 minutes until lightly browned and cooked through.

Remove from the oven and serve with red onion rings and lime wedges to squeeze over.

fish
dishes

kerala-style fish
steamed in banana leaves

serves 4
each serving is:
Free on Extra Easy
Free on Original
7 Syns on Green

ready in 20 minutes plus marinating

4 thick white fish fillets (cod, halibut or monkfish), skinless

4 large pieces of banana leaf or baking parchment

110g coriander leaves, chopped

5 tbsp chopped mint

1 onion, peeled and chopped

1 tsp peeled and finely grated root ginger

2 green chillies, deseeded and finely chopped

finely grated zest and juice of 1 large lime

salt and freshly ground black pepper

Pat the fish dry with kitchen paper and place on a plate. Heat each banana leaf (if using) over an open flame until it turns bright green and becomes supple. Remove and set aside.

Put the chopped coriander and mint, onion, ginger, green chillies, lime zest and juice in a food processor. Season well, add a little water and blend until fairly smooth. Spread this mixture over the fish, cover and allow to marinate for 10-12 minutes.

Place a large steamer over a pan of simmering water. Lay one piece of fish on each banana leaf (or baking parchment) with some marinade and wrap up to make a parcel enclosing the fish. Secure with small skewers and place the parcels in the steamer (you may have to do this in batches), cover and cook for 8-10 minutes or until the fish is opaque and cooked through.

Carefully remove the parcels from the steamer and unwrap at the table so that everyone can savour the aroma. Serve with kachumber, if wished, see recipe on page 36.

Tip: *You can bake the fish instead of steaming it. Simply place on a non-stick baking sheet and bake at 190°C/Gas 5 for 10-15 minutes.*

tandoori
monkfish

serves 4
each serving is:
Free on Extra Easy
Free on Original
5 Syns on Green

ready in 25 minutes plus marinating

4 x 150g monkfish tail fillets

150g fat free natural yogurt

3 garlic cloves, peeled and crushed

1 tsp peeled and grated root ginger

1 tbsp tandoori spice powder

juice of 1 lemon

salt and freshly ground black pepper

for the salad

1 small cucumber

1 small red onion, peeled

4 ripe plum tomatoes

2 tbsp chopped coriander

1 tsp chopped mint

juice of 1 lime

Rinse the fish fillets and pat dry with kitchen paper. In a large bowl, mix the yogurt with the garlic, ginger, tandoori spice powder and lemon juice. Season well.

Add the fish to the yogurt mixture and toss gently to coat. Cover and leave to marinate in the fridge for at least 3 hours (or overnight if time permits).

Preheat the oven to 200°C/Gas 6. Line a baking sheet with baking parchment. Lift the fish from the marinade and place on the baking sheet in a single layer. Bake for 12-15 minutes or until cooked through.

While the fish is cooking, prepare the salad. Peel, halve and deseed the cucumber. Cut the cucumber, onion and tomatoes into 1.5cm dice and place in a bowl. Add the chopped herbs and lime juice and season to taste. Toss to mix well.

Place the monkfish fillets on serving plates and accompany with the salad.

Tip: You can use any firm-fleshed white fish in place of the monkfish, if preferred.

chilli-spiced squid

700g fresh squid, cleaned and cut into bite-sized rings or pieces

2 tsp sea salt

juice of 2 lemons

1 tsp ground coriander

1 tsp ground cumin

1 tsp hot chilli powder

1 level tsp tomato purée

1 red chilli, deseeded and finely sliced

1 tsp peeled and finely grated root ginger

1 garlic clove, peeled and crushed

low calorie cooking spray

a large handful of chopped coriander

1 small red onion, peeled and very thinly sliced

a small handful of chopped mint

Place the squid in a bowl and in another bowl, mix together the sea salt, lemon juice, ground spices, chilli powder, tomato purée, red chilli, ginger and garlic. Pour this mixture over the squid. Toss to coat evenly, cover and allow to stand at room temperature for 12-15 minutes.

Spray a pan with low calorie cooking spray and place over a very high heat. Working in batches, lift the squid from the marinade and sear in the hot pan for 2-3 minutes. Remove and keep warm in a serving bowl while you repeat the steps for the remaining squid.

Stir the chopped coriander, red onion and chopped mint through the cooked squid, toss to mix well and eat immediately.

tamarind
and salmon curry

serves 4
each serving is:
3 Syns on Extra Easy
3 Syns on Original
19½ Syns on Green

freezer friendly
ready in 20 minutes

low calorie cooking spray

2 garlic cloves, peeled and thinly sliced

2 tsp cumin seeds

1 tsp each of black mustard seeds and
crushed coriander seeds

12-15 fresh curry leaves

750g salmon fillet, skinned and cut into
bite-sized pieces

2 level tbsp tomato purée

¼ tbsp artificial sweetener

1 tsp each of garam masala and
ground cumin

8 tbsp finely chopped coriander

2 red chillies, deseeded and finely sliced

2 level tsp tamarind paste*

200ml reduced fat coconut milk

salt

Spray a large saucepan with low calorie cooking spray and place over a medium heat. Add the garlic, cumin seeds, mustard seeds, coriander seeds and curry leaves and stir-fry for 1-2 minutes.

Add the salmon to the pan. Mix the remaining ingredients together (except the salt) and pour into the pan. Turn the heat to medium-low. Cover and allow the mixture to simmer and cook for 6-8 minutes or until the fish is cooked through.

Remove the pan from the heat, season well with salt and serve immediately.

Tamarind paste is available in larger supermarkets, but if you can't find it, use the juice of a lemon or lime instead.

rice, lentils & pulses

spinach dhal

serves 4
each serving is:
Free on Extra Easy
Free on Green
9½ Syns on Original

freezer friendly
vegetarian
ready in 40 minutes

250g dried yellow split lentils, rinsed
and drained

200g baby leaf spinach,
roughly chopped

low calorie cooking spray

4 shallots, peeled and very finely chopped

1 tsp peeled and finely chopped
root ginger

2 red chillies, deseeded and finely sliced

8-10 fresh curry leaves

½ tsp turmeric

4 plum tomatoes, roughly chopped

salt

Place the lentils in a saucepan with 700ml of hot water and bring to the boil, skimming off any scum that comes to the surface. Reduce the heat to medium-low and cook for 20-25 minutes, stirring often to ensure that the thickened lentils don't stick to the bottom of the pan.

Add the spinach, stir, cover and cook gently for 5-6 minutes.

Meanwhile, spray a frying pan with low calorie cooking spray and place over a medium heat. Add the shallots and stir-fry for 4-5 minutes and then add the ginger, red chillies and curry leaves. Stir-fry for 2-3 minutes, add the turmeric and stir. Scrape the contents of the frying pan into the lentils, add the tomatoes and cook on a medium heat for 4-5 minutes. Season well and serve immediately.

chana
masala

serves 4
each serving is:
Free on Extra Easy
Free on Green
7½ Syns on Original

freezer friendly
vegetarian
ready in 30 minutes

low calorie cooking spray

1 cinnamon stick

3cm piece root ginger, peeled and
cut into thin shreds

6 garlic cloves, peeled and crushed

1 green chilli, deseeded and thinly sliced

1 small onion, peeled and finely chopped

1 tbsp medium curry powder

110g passata

1 large potato, peeled and cut into cubes

400g can chickpeas, drained and rinsed

a squeeze of lemon juice

¼ tsp garam masala

salt

2 tbsp each of chopped mint
and coriander

Spray a large frying pan with low calorie cooking spray and place over a medium heat. Add the cinnamon stick, ginger, garlic and most of the green chilli and stir-fry for 1 minute. Add the onion and cook for 6-7 minutes or until softened.

Add the curry powder and stir-fry for 1 minute then add the passata, the potatoes and 150ml of hot water. Stir and bring to the boil, cover and reduce the heat to low. Cook gently for 10-12 minutes and then add the chickpeas and cook for 5 minutes or until the potatoes are tender.

Remove from the heat, sprinkle over the lemon juice and garam masala, season well and stir in the chopped herbs. Serve garnished with the remaining green chilli.

mixed bean
and carrot bhaji

low calorie cooking spray

1 tsp cumin seeds

1 small onion, peeled and finely chopped

2 garlic cloves, peeled and finely chopped

1 tsp peeled and finely grated root ginger

1 green chilli, deseeded and sliced

1 tomato, roughly chopped

2 tsp mild curry powder

200g carrots, peeled and cut into thick
batons, boiled and drained

200g green beans, trimmed, halved,
boiled and drained

200g can butter beans, rinsed and drained

salt

4 tbsp finely chopped coriander

Spray a large frying pan with low calorie cooking spray and place over a medium heat. Add the cumin seeds, onion, garlic, ginger and green chilli and stir-fry for 4-5 minutes.

Turn the heat to high and add the tomato, curry powder and 150ml of water. Stir and cook for 2-3 minutes.

Add the carrots, green beans and butter beans and cook for a further 3-4 minutes. Remove from the heat, season well and stir in the chopped coriander before serving.

gobi chawal

serves 4
each serving is:
Free on Extra Easy
Free on Green
8½ Syns on Original

freezer friendly
vegetarian
ready in 20 minutes

low calorie cooking spray

2 tbsp peeled and finely chopped
red onion

1 cinnamon stick

1 bay leaf

3 cardamom pods, crushed

1 tsp cumin seeds

2 cloves

200g each of boiled cauliflower and
broccoli florets

500g boiled brown or
white basmati rice

salt and freshly ground black pepper

Spray a large wok with low calorie cooking spray and place over a high heat. Add the red onion, cinnamon stick, bay leaf, cardamom pods, cumin seeds and cloves and stir-fry for 3-4 minutes.

Add the cauliflower and broccoli florets and stir-fry for 1-2 minutes.

Add the cooked rice and stir-fry over a high heat for 4-5 minutes or until piping hot. Season and serve immediately.

biryani

serves 4
each serving is:
Free on Extra Easy
Free on Green
8 Syns on Original

vegetarian
ready in 20 minutes

225g Quorn Mince

low calorie cooking spray

4 spring onions, thinly sliced

1 garlic clove, peeled and finely chopped

2.5cm piece root ginger, peeled
and grated

1 egg

450g freshly boiled basmati rice

110g frozen mixed vegetables

1 tbsp soy sauce

freshly ground black pepper

Fry the mince in a little low calorie cooking spray for 4-5 minutes. Meanwhile, in another pan, fry the spring onions, garlic and ginger for 1-2 minutes. Crack in the egg and scramble for a couple of minutes until the egg is just set.

Stir the mince, rice and mixed vegetables into the spring onion mixture and continue to cook for a further 4-5 minutes until piping hot.

Stir in the soy sauce and add black pepper to taste. Serve immediately.

root vegetable
biryani

serves 4
each serving is:
Free on Extra Easy
Free on Green
24½ Syns on Original

vegetarian
ready in 45 minutes

1 onion, peeled and chopped

2 medium potatoes, peeled and chopped

2 medium sweet potatoes, peeled and chopped

1 swede, peeled and chopped

2 garlic cloves, peeled and crushed

4 carrots, peeled and sliced

4 medium parsnips, peeled and sliced

1 tbsp medium curry powder

1 tbsp chat masala*

350g dried rice

chopped coriander, to serve

Place the onion, potatoes, swede, garlic, carrots and parsnips in a large pan. Cover with 900ml of boiling water, bring to the boil, reduce the heat and simmer for 15 minutes.

Add the curry powder and chat masala, stir and cook for a further 2 minutes. Add the rice and, stirring often, cook for 20 minutes until the rice is cooked and the liquid has been absorbed.

Serve sprinkled with chopped coriander.

See Aloo Chat recipe on page 28.

pilau rice

serves 4
each serving is:
Free on Extra Easy
Free on Green
20½ Syns on Original

freezer friendly
vegetarian
ready in 35 minutes plus soaking

450g dried basmati rice

low calorie cooking spray

1 medium onion, peeled and
finely chopped

6 cardamom pods

8 cloves

6 peppercorns

1 cinnamon stick

a small pinch of saffron threads

2 bay leaves

600ml hot vegetable stock or water

salt

Wash the rice in several changes of cold water, then leave to soak in fresh cold water for about 30 minutes.

Spray a medium sized non-stick saucepan with low calorie cooking spray and place over a medium heat. Cook the onion for about 5 minutes until softened.

Add the spices, saffron threads and bay leaves and cook for further 2 minutes. The spices will give a wonderful fragrant flavour to the rice.

Drain the rice, add to the pan and stir until the grains are coated in the spice mixture. Stir in the stock or water and season with salt. Bring to the boil and then cover with a tight-fitting lid.

Turn the heat down to low and leave to cook for 10 minutes before turning off the heat. Don't remove the lid; just leave the rice to continue cooking in the pan for about 10 minutes until you're ready to serve.

Fluff up the grains before serving.

vegetable
dishes

spiced beetroot
with coconut

serves 4
each serving is:
2 Syns on Extra Easy
2 Syns on Green
2 Syns on Original

freezer friendly
vegetarian
ready in 15 minutes

low calorie cooking spray

2 garlic cloves, peeled and crushed

1 tsp peeled and finely grated root ginger

2 tsp cumin seeds

1 tsp coriander seeds, roughly crushed

1 dried red chilli, roughly crushed

700g beetroot, freshly cooked, peeled and cut into thick slices

150ml reduced fat coconut milk

juice of 1 lime

zest of 1 lime, finely grated

¼ tsp ground cardamom seeds

a small handful of fresh coriander, chopped

salt

Spray a large non-stick frying pan or wok with low calorie cooking spray and place over a high heat.

Add the garlic, ginger, cumin and coriander seeds, and red chilli and stir fry for 1-2 minutes.

Add the beetroot and stir-fry for 1-2 minutes. Then add the coconut milk, the juice and zest of the lime and the ground cardamom seeds. Cook for 2-3 minutes and remove from the heat. Stir in the chopped coriander, season with salt and serve immediately.

sabzi
kari

serves 4
each serving is:
1 Syn on Extra Easy
1 Syn on Green
1½ Syns on Original

freezer friendly
vegetarian
ready in 25 minutes

low calorie cooking spray

2 green chillies, deseeded and
finely chopped

1 tsp peeled and finely grated ginger

2 tsp ground cumin

1 tsp black peppercorns, crushed

1 tsp ground cinnamon

1 tsp ground cardamom seeds

a pinch of grated nutmeg

200g butternut squash, peeled,
deseeded and cubed

200g courgettes, cut into chunks

25g frozen peas

150g fat free natural yogurt

150ml vegetable stock

salt

1 level tbsp flaked almonds, to serve

Spray a large non-stick frying pan with low calorie cooking spray and place over a medium heat. Add the green chillies and ginger and stir-fry for 2-3 minutes. Add the remaining spices and stir-fry for a further 2-3 minutes.

Add the vegetables and stir-fry for 3-4 minutes.

Blend the yogurt with the stock and add to the pan. Stir, cover and cook gently for 10-12 minutes (do not allow to boil), or until the vegetables are just tender. Season and garnish with the flaked almonds. This dish is equally delicious with vegetables such as aubergine, potato, carrots or cauliflower, choose your favourites.

sweetcorn
and red pepper bhaji

serves 4
each serving is:
Free on Extra Easy
Free on Green
3½ Syns on Original

freezer friendly
vegetarian
ready in 25 minutes

2 corn on the cob

low calorie cooking spray

1 small onion, peeled and finely chopped

2 red peppers, deseeded and
cut into 2cm cubes

1 green chilli, cut in half lengthways and
deseeded (optional)

6-8 fresh curry leaves

1 tsp ground coriander

250g tomatoes, chopped

¼ tsp artificial sweetener

3 tbsp finely chopped coriander

1 tsp garam masala

salt

Using a sharp knife, strip the corn kernels off the cob, put into a bowl and set aside.

Spray a large non-stick frying pan with low calorie cooking spray and place over a medium heat. Add the onion and stir-fry for 4-5 minutes until softened.

Add the sweetcorn, red peppers, green chilli, curry leaves and ground coriander and stir-fry for 2 minutes. Then add the tomatoes and sweetener, stir, cover and cook gently for 8-10 minutes.

Remove the frying pan from the heat and stir in the chopped coriander and garam masala. Season well and serve immediately.

khumbi
curry and rice

serves 4
each serving is:
Free on Extra Easy
Free on Green
10½ Syns on Original

freezer friendly
vegetarian
ready in 20 minutes

200g dried white rice

2 tsp peeled and finely grated root ginger

110g peeled and finely grated onion

4 garlic cloves, peeled and crushed

low calorie cooking spray

500g large button mushrooms,
halved or quartered

3 tbsp fat free natural yogurt

1 level tbsp tomato purée

2 tsp ground coriander

1 tsp mild chilli powder

175g frozen peas

salt and freshly ground black pepper

4 tbsp chopped coriander

Cook the rice according to the packet instructions, drain and keep warm.

Meanwhile, mix together the ginger, onion and garlic with 4 tablespoons of water in a small bowl and set aside.

Spray a large non-stick wok with low calorie cooking spray and place over a high heat. Add the mushrooms and stir-fry for 5-6 minutes or until lightly browned. Transfer the mushrooms to a bowl and set aside. Wipe the wok with kitchen paper and re-spray with low calorie cooking spray.

Place over a high heat and add the onion mixture. Stir-fry for 3-4 minutes and then add the yogurt, 1 tablespoon at a time. Add the tomato purée and ground coriander and stir-fry for 1 minute before adding 300ml of water, the mushrooms with juices and the chilli powder.

Add the peas to a pan of lightly salted boiling water, cover and bring back to the boil. Simmer for 3-4 minutes, drain and keep warm.

Season the mushroom mixture well and simmer gently for 5-6 minutes (do not allow to boil). Remove from the heat and stir in the chopped coriander. Serve with the rice and peas.

gobi chana curry

serves 4
each serving is:
Free on Extra Easy
Free on Green
14 Syns on Original

freezer friendly
vegetarian
ready in 30 minutes

low calorie cooking spray

8 spring onions, cut into short lengths

2 garlic cloves, peeled and crushed

2 tsp ground ginger

2 tsp mild curry powder

1 red pepper and 1 green pepper, deseeded
and cut into bite-sized chunks

300g cauliflower, separated into small florets

500g passata

1 tsp artificial sweetener

400g can chickpeas, drained and rinsed

salt and freshly ground black pepper

450g boiled rice, fat free natural yogurt
and chopped mint, to serve

Spray a pan with low calorie cooking spray and cook the spring onions for 2-3 minutes. Add the garlic, ginger and curry powder and stir quickly. Then add the peppers and cauliflower and cook for a further 2-3 minutes.

Stir in the passata and sweetener and bring to the boil. Cover, reduce the heat, and cook for 10 minutes, stirring occasionally. Add the chickpeas, season well and bring to the boil.

Remove from the heat and serve with freshly boiled rice, drizzled with yogurt and garnished with chopped mint.

aloo gobi

serves 4
each serving is:
Free on Extra Easy
Free on Green
3½ Syns on Original

freezer friendly
vegetarian
ready in 35 minutes

low calorie cooking spray

1 onion, peeled and finely chopped

2 tsp cumin seeds

2 large potatoes, peeled and cut into
bite-sized cubes

1 head of cauliflower, separated into
bite-sized florets

1 tsp mild or medium chilli powder

½ tsp turmeric

2 tsp ground coriander

2 tsp garam masala

2 tsp amchoor (dried mango powder)*

salt

chopped coriander and mint, to serve

Spray a large non-stick wok with low calorie cooking spray and place over a medium heat. Add the onion to the wok and stir-fry for 4-5 minutes until softened. Add the cumin seeds and stir-fry for a further 2-3 minutes.

Add the potatoes and cauliflower and stir-fry over a high heat for 4-5 minutes. Add the chilli powder, turmeric, ground coriander, garam masala and amchoor and stir-fry for 2-3 minutes.

Pour in 200ml of water and season well. Cover and cook gently for 10-15 minutes, or until the cauliflower and potatoes are tender. Season to taste.

Remove from the heat and serve garnished with the chopped herbs.

Amchoor is available from larger supermarkets and Asian greengrocers.

spinach and sweet potato curry

serves 4
each serving is:
Free on Extra Easy
Free on Green
8 Syns on Original

freezer friendly
vegetarian
ready in 35 minutes

300ml vegetable stock

750g sweet potatoes, peeled and cut into
bite-sized wedges

1 onion, peeled, halved and thinly sliced

225g baby leaf spinach

2 garlic cloves, peeled and thinly sliced

1 red chilli, deseeded and thinly sliced

1 tbsp medium or hot curry powder

4 ripe plum tomatoes, chopped

salt and freshly ground black pepper

Place the stock in a large saucepan and add the sweet potatoes and onions. Bring to the boil, reduce the heat, cover and cook gently for 4-5 minutes.

Add the spinach, garlic, red chilli, curry powder and tomatoes to the pan, stir well and cook over a medium heat for 10 minutes or until the spinach has just wilted and the potatoes are tender. Season well and serve hot.

bombay
potatoes

serves 4
each serving is:
Free on Extra Easy
Free on Green
8 Syns on Original

freezer friendly
vegetarian
ready in 40 minutes

low calorie cooking spray

1 tsp black mustard seeds

1 tsp ground cumin

1 tsp turmeric

1 tsp ground coriander

1 tsp garam masala

1 tsp chilli powder

2 tsp peeled and finely chopped root ginger

6 medium potatoes, peeled, parboiled and cut into cubes

4 tomatoes, cores removed and flesh diced

4 tbsp roughly chopped coriander

Spray a large, non-stick pan with low calorie cooking spray, place over a medium heat and fry the mustard seeds, ground cumin, turmeric, ground coriander, garam masala, chilli powder and ginger for a few minutes.

Add the potatoes, making sure they are completely coated in the spicy mixture.

Stir-fry for about 10-15 minutes, then stir in the tomatoes and coriander. Cook for 1-2 minutes and remove from the heat. Serve immediately.

desserts

baked figs
with almond 'cream'

serves 4
each serving is:
2½ Syns on Extra Easy
2½ Syns on Green
2½ Syns on Original

vegetarian
ready in 20 minutes

8 ripe figs

low calorie cooking spray

1 tbsp ground cinnamon

3 tbsp artificial sweetener

a pinch of cinnamon, to dust

for the almond 'cream'
100g quark

150g fat free natural fromage frais

a few drops of almond essence

Preheat the oven to 200°C/Gas 6. Cut the figs in half through the middle of the stalk. Place cut side up on a baking dish and spray with low calorie cooking spray. Dust with the cinnamon and 1 tablespoon of the sweetener and bake for 10-12 minutes.

Meanwhile, make the almond 'cream': whisk together the quark and fromage frais, add the almond essence and remaining sweetener and mix until combined.

Remove the figs from the oven, divide between four plates, top with the almond 'cream' and serve dusted with cinnamon.

creamy
mango sorbet

serves 4
each serving is:
2½ **Syns** on Extra Easy
2½ **Syns** on Green
2½ **Syns** on Original

freezer friendly
ready in 10 minutes plus freezing

350g fresh mango, peeled and
stoned, plus slices to garnish

2-3 tbsp artificial sweetener

190g pot Vanilla Müllerlight Yogurt

Place the mango flesh in a food processor with the sweetener and yogurt. Blend until smooth, then pour into a freezer-proof container.

Freeze for 2-3 hours or until the sides and base of the sorbet have started to set but the centre is still liquid. Beat the mixture with a fork and then return to the freezer for 4-5 hours, or until firm, beating every 30-40 minutes to break up the ice crystals.

Transfer the sorbet to the fridge for 10-15 minutes before scooping into bowls. Serve garnished with fresh mango slices.

vanilla-spiced plums

serves 4
each serving is:
5 Syns on Extra Easy
5 Syns on Green
5 Syns on Original

freezer friendly
vegetarian
ready in 25 minutes plus overnight chilling

2 vanilla pods

12 plums

125ml red wine

250ml diluted sugar-free blackcurrant squash

2 cinnamon sticks

2 cloves

1 tsp ground cinnamon

1 level tbsp golden caster sugar

6-8 tbsp artificial sweetener

Split the vanilla pods and place in a pan with all the other ingredients. Place over a medium heat and bring to the boil. Cover, reduce the heat and simmer gently for 6-8 minutes or until the plums are just tender.

Remove from the heat and take out the plums with a slotted spoon. Peel and transfer to a serving dish. Strain the syrup into a jug.

Pour the syrup over the plums, cover and chill overnight to let the flavours develop.

Serve the plums straight from the fridge, or warm through first in a pan.

peach and cardamom brûlée

serves 4
each serving is:
3 Syns on Extra Easy
3 Syns on Green
3 Syns on Original

vegetarian
ready in 20-25 minutes

2 x 150g pots Total 0% Fat
Greek Natural Yogurt

2-3 cardamon pods

a few drops of vanilla essence

3-4 tbsp artificial sweetener

900g ripe peaches, peeled, stoned
and finely chopped

4 level tbsp caster sugar

Place the yogurt in a mixing bowl. Peel the skin from the cardamom pods and carefully remove the black seeds. Place the seeds in a mortar and crush with a pestle until fine. Alternatively, place them on a board and crush with a rolling pin. Stir into the yogurt along with the vanilla essence and sweetener.

Divide the chopped peaches between four individual glass ramekins and top with the yogurt mixture. Sprinkle over the caster sugar.

Heat a grill to medium-high. Place the ramekins on a rack under the grill for 5-6 minutes until the top is golden and slightly caramelised. Allow to cool slightly before serving.

lemon and apricot delight

serves 4
each serving is:
2½ Syns on Extra Easy
2½ Syns on Green
2½ Syns on Original

vegetarian
ready in 15 minutes plus chilling

600g apricots, peeled and sliced

2 tbsp artificial sweetener (or to taste)

1 tbsp lemon juice

2 large egg whites*

4 tbsp fat free natural fromage frais

ground cinnamon, to dust

Place most of the apricots in a pan with 150ml of water and half of the sweetener and simmer for 6-7 minutes until tender. Transfer to a food processor and blend to a purée. Allow to cool, then stir in the lemon juice.

Meanwhile, whisk the egg whites until softly peaked and then gradually whisk in the remaining sweetener until shiny and stiff. Divide half of the apricot purée between four chilled glasses and carefully fold the rest into the egg white mixture. Top up the glasses with the egg white mixture and chilli in the fridge for 2-3 hours.

Garnish with the remaining apricot slices, a spoonful of fromage frais and a dusting of cinnamon and serve immediately.

Pregnant women, the elderly and babies are advised not to eat raw eggs.

pistachio and
ginger ice

serves 4
each serving is:
5 Syns on Extra Easy
5 Syns on Green
5 Syns on Original

freezer friendly
vegetarian
ready in 10 minutes plus freezing

4 pieces stem ginger in syrup, drained
and finely chopped

4 level dsp chopped pistachio nuts

500g fat free natural fromage frais

2-3 tbsp artificial sweetener

a few drops of green food
colouring (optional)

Mix most of the chopped ginger and chopped nuts in a bowl with the other ingredients.

Transfer the mixture to a shallow freezer-proof container and freeze for 4 hours or until firm, stirring every 30 minutes to prevent ice crystals forming.

To serve, scoop the ice cream into bowls and garnish with the remaining chopped ginger and nuts.

index

aloo chat 28

aloo gobi 98

baked figs with almond 'cream' 106

beef kofta curry 32

beef madras 34

biryani 80

bombay potatoes 102

chana masala 74

chicken tikka masala 52

chilli-spiced squid 64

classic chicken curry 46

coconut chicken soup 8

creamy chicken korma 54

creamy mango sorbet 108

curried parsnip soup 10

dahiwalla ghosht with kachumber 36

gobi chana curry 96

gobi chawal 78

grilled tiger prawns 16

jalfrezi chicken 48

kerala-style fish steamed in banana leaves 60

kheema with curry leaves 42

khumbi curry and rice 94

lamb dhansak 40

lamb koftas with mint relish 12

lamb rogan josh 38

lemon and apricot delight 114

lemon grass prawn salad 26

masala crab cakes 18

meaty citrus salad 24

mixed bean and carrot bhaji 76

onion bhajis 20

peach and cardamom brûlée 112

pilau rice 84

pistachio and ginger ice 116

pork vindaloo 44

root vegetable biryani 82

sabzi kari 90

shahi murgh 50

speedy prawn curry 66

spiced beetroot with coconut 88

spinach and sweet potato curry 100

spinach dhal 72

sweetcorn and red pepper bhaji 92

tamarind and salmon curry 68

tandoori chicken 14

tandoori monkfish 62

turkey shami kebabs 56

vanilla-spiced plums 110

vegetable samosas with hara chutney 22

conversions

We have used metric measurements throughout this book. If you prefer to use imperial measurements, the following lists will help you.

grams/ounces

25g	1oz
50g	2oz
60g	2½oz
75g	3oz
100g	3½oz
110g	4oz (¼lb)
150g	5oz
175g	6oz
200g	7oz
225g	8oz (½lb)
250g	9oz
275g	10oz
300g	11oz
350g	12oz (¾lb)
375g	13oz
400g	14oz
425g	15oz
450g	16oz (1lb)
500g	18oz (1lb 2oz)
550g	20oz (1lb 4oz)
600g	22oz (1lb 6oz)
700g	24oz (1lb 8oz)
750g	26oz (1lb 10oz)
800g	28oz (1lb 12oz)
850g	30oz (1lb 14oz)
900g	32oz (2lb)
1000g/1kg	36oz (2lb 4oz)

millilitres/fluid ounces/pints

50ml	2fl oz
75ml	3fl oz
100ml	3½fl oz
125ml	4fl oz
150ml	5fl oz (¼ pint)
200ml	7fl oz
250ml	9fl oz
300ml	11fl oz
400ml	14fl oz
450ml	16fl oz
600ml	20fl oz (1 pint)
700ml	24fl oz (1¼ pints)
900ml	30fl oz (1½ pints)
1 litre	35fl oz (1¾ pints)
1.2 litres	40fl oz (2 pints)
1.4 litres	48fl oz (2½ pints)
2 litres	70fl oz (3½ pints)

centimetres/inches

1.5cm	½ inch
2cm	¾ inch
2.5cm	1 inch
3cm	1½ inches